Seven Ways to Clean the Air

by Jack Garman

Summer, 2023

You'll save the planet and
you will, too.
And you will and you will
and so will you and you.

It's easy for all of us
to each be themselves
in the strong and straining protest
'gainst the vague and changing documents

they tie us to,

as if a new-fresh terminology

will bring us any closer

to a clean and fresh-aired planet for all.

It's easy for a lot of us

to make it known to few of them

that we want certain things

to be done right away.

We know the sky is dying,

slowly, quickly, just in time.

So once we pick a passion,

to give the sky a second chance,

another fresh breath,

once we aim en masse

to chain and restrain

any vast and global enterprise
that kicks out carbon
at a choke-us-out pace,
once we pick a certain target,
make it clear what we want,
we've got a better chance
to clean the air.

Its easiest to do it
through the topmost eco orgs.
They have endless sheets
of pressure-sensitive labels
with pressure-sensitive names
and they know how to get
the point across.

So far, when all you do is

change the carbon terms,
push back and back the date,
and pay a global fine or fee,
its more like a gambit of
globalized accounting
where the carbon in the air
gets reassigned
to a fast-receding column
in a deep-away row.
So what do you think
will happen to us all
when we finally do fill in
that empty spreadsheet cell
so far, far away?

Only then will we truly know
that our vast atmosphere

can't expand, can't grow,
can't spreadsheet itself
to leap beyond tomorrow,
while we pivot and parry
this wispy output to another column
on a government form.
Only once we pivot to the final sheet
and burrow our way
across the bottom row
where we finally downtally
the last breath we have
and hey, it's pure co2.

Only then do we
come to realize that
net-zero is not zero.

Maybe now is the time

to find a way

to ease this gasping misery.

First Thing We Do is Practical As Air

First, it really is so easy
to plant trees in forest numbers
wherever they already grow.

One trillion ought to do it,
from what I hear,
not so big a number
with many hands at work.

Get those trillion planted,
anywhere they belong,

anywhere they already grow.

Let the mighty trillion
with all their lovely leaves
drink down all the luscious co2.

Let the thirsty trillion
drink it all down
with any kind of
help we can give.

Yet surely notice something
all you planters o' the trees.
Take note of what happens
when we plant those trillion trees
and all along the way
we steadily stack up

extra carbon on top
of what we kick out now.

And know this too,
you planters 'o the trees
that those lovely trees
will help us the most
some thirty years away
once they truly leaf out
their magnificent leaf acreage.

They'll help, of course,
to cleanse the carbon stacks
we store in the sky.
They'll help each day they grow,
but they'll truly help the most
with our problems of today

thirty years downstream.

Yet, all the way along,
we add extra carbon to the air
by machines we use for planting,
by machines we use
for replacing all the ones
that don't make it.
Trucks and tillers and every sort of gear
in use for years and years,
and then in use
for years and years more.

Makes me have to think
that once we get
that happy trillion
put into the ground,

we'll need a trillion more
to clean up behind us,
in a deadly race to a finish line
neither we nor the future
can see.

It should be clear by now that
every solution
adds extra pollution.

It should be clear by now that
when we all look again
at the problem of the sky
everyone can see that
net–zero is not zero.

Sure, let's plant a trillion trees

and let's plant them each by hand
to avoid all the carbon
that comes from the planting
of magnificent trees.

Plant a trillion trees
wherever you can grow them since,
we know we'll need them all,
thirty years down.

Plant those trillion trees
without burning fuel,
anywhere trees grow.

Your yard, if you have one.
Your village plot, if you have one.
Edge of town, if you have one.

Plant whatever grows
and plant the most you can.

Then plant some more
when you're done.

A trillion is a long way off,
and the way things are going,
we might need
a trillion more
when we're finally
totally done.

Give it seven years
at hand-planting speed.

Remember all planters,
great green ideas
put out extra carbon,
all add to the carbon
stacked up on our heads.

Every bit of that
terrific progress,
every great new tech that cuts
warm co2,
lays an extra layer on top
of the wreck we already have.

We're happy with everything
they promise us in writing
so, sure, we barrel on.

But, oh, the earth gets worse,
the earth gets so much worse
that year after year
we race and we race,
faster and smarter and
more to the point,
to the point where
we choke ourselves out.

Every solution
adds extra pollution
like little cat footprints
in multiple millions.

Every solution
adds extra pollution,
everything we try

makes it worse all along.

We don't want to think
we're in the first loops
of a global death spiral,
a centrifuge of more and more speed,
where we choke ourselves out one day.

We need to realize,
everywhere realize,
each of us, all of us, too
that the only thing
that adds nothing
to the carbon
stacked on our heads
is nothing.

Second Thing We Do
        We Fall in Love With Very Slowly

Beyond the growing forests,
the next thing we do,
how easy it is,
like a switch on a wall in your home,
is to simply turn off
all civil aviation
around the world
for the next seven years.

All we have to do

is pause every pertinent permit
for the next seven years.

The owners might object,
they have that right.
They can launch a suit
that will work it's way through
for the next seven years.

That little Piper owner might say
"I don't pollute a lot."
Of course you don't,
little Piper owner.

No one pollutes a lot.

But remember,

little Piper owner,
everyone pollutes a lot.

Every single-engine,
every elegant airliner,
every puddle-jumper,
every cargo hauler,
every bi-plane,
tri-plane, monoplane,
every civilian airplane,
known or yet to be,
grounded for the next seven years
while we make our way
about the earth
without them.

We did just fine

before Kitty Hawk.

We did just fine before we flew.

We'll do just fine once we
drop our wings and
walk again.

And oh, do we love airplanes,
those sleek transits of the sky.

They fly so fast,
they fly so high,
they fly our goods
and they fly ourselves
to every corner of the world,
and they do it dirtier

than any other way
we already have.

Dirtier than trucks and cars,
dirtier than bikes and trains.

A polluted atmosphere
is the price we pay
for those sleek transits of the sky.

A polluted atmosphere
is the price we pay for speed.

Whatever future tech we have,
whatever tech is coming down the chute
we can pause civilian airplanes
for the next seven years,

make room in the carbon stack
for any new-tech carbon yet to come.

Suspend the permits,
let the lawyers fly
their paper planes
for the next seven years.

We can punch a hole
in the carbon stack
before we choke ourselves out.

Drop half the carbon
out of the sky,
drop it down to 300 ppm,
for a year and half
and we might have a chance

to benefit from unseen new tech

before we choke ourselves out.

Third Thing We Do Might Hurt a Bit

This is where we call upon
Generation AA,
The Battery People
to break themselves loose from
the global grasp of Greta.

Maybe there's someone
who wants to build a better carbon trap
or other technology of note.

Maybe there's someone who
wants to earn some money for themselves

and their struggling families.

Maybe there's some who are content
to play a game
or who largely ignore this call.

But what would it mean if they
all agreed with Greta, not a single
word of their own?
It's an eerie land of silence where
youthful thinkers all agree.

Many must have more to say
than these few lines convey.

Many must have more to say
than Greta has to say.

Generation AA,
The Battery People
deserve more than one Greta.

Maybe they should get a chance
to say what they themselves think.
Something more than 'Greta,
Oh Greta, Great Greta, My Greta.'

Fourth Thing We Do Is So Very Global

For the next seven years,
Every City a Dark Sky City.

The beautiful cities of the world
openly and strongly display
their magnificent splendor
at sunrise, at sunset,
but bosh they are so garish
when lit up at night.

Floodlights everywhere,

lights on top of lights,
and all of it is visible from space.

You've seen the spacey-cool pics
of Mother Earth at night.
Cities lit up, highways stretched
like webs of light.
That's really nothing more
than wasted electricity,
so much waste it's
visible from space.
The future of the human race
burned off all night long.

Instead, look at every city skyline
while the sun slowly rises, slowly sets.

Mother Nature has her way
with her colors as the palette shifts,
oh so slowly shifts,
her angled yellow beams
that turn soft orange
slide into ruddy reds,
become plump purples,
silent and exotic, raging softly
on first a single glass pane,
then a stone column,
then a strip of polished rock.

Stone columns, stone rows
change color, shift texture,
oh so slowly
you can't track it,
right before your eyes.

The work of nature
and the hand of man on display,
a transformation leisurely and passionate,
the graceful, raging sun,
every moment on the move
 movement nearly always imperceptible,
a graceful spectacle free to all.

Silently, elegantly, gracefully,
the sun rises, the sun sets
as human lights release
and grab the scene.

By silent command the evening lights begin
their incandescent immolations
in a heavy-metal nightmare,

a buzzing, popping, scheming
collision of crude ideas,
the desperation of flickering,
ghoulish urban miserablism.

Your tax dollars in dispirited dispute
with your tax dollars.

The elegant urban landscape
is slapped into slabs
of ghoulish green, cold blue white,
floodlit scraggly crags
of pointless overwhelm.

Worst of all,
exquisite day-built architecture
is wiped from human memory.

Where is the graceful curve of light,
the smattering of colors
that give and take from one night to the next?

Who can tell what day it is
when the nightscape looks the same
every night?

Stars are forgotten,
the moon a steampunk postcard.

For the next seven years,
let urban cityscapes serve
as canvases for art.

Let urban artists work with inky black

and every kind of light.

Let the nightly urban sky
restate the marching of the days,
and give off seven years less co2.

Let seven lightscapes change each day
and keep the juice down
to a crucial safety level.

We don't need to flood every building
in cheap, cold glare.
Let the artists use the cities
as vast canvases of light.
Let the nightly carbon drop,
we'll have a different view
of where we live.

Take it easy on the air

for the next seven years,

give us all a chance to nightly see

our personal global architecture

that changes every night

like a sprawling calendar.

Fifth Massive Cleanse of Our Air

No planes in the air.

Once we do without them
for seven long years,
we'll know by then
how much our sky will clear.

Our sky might clear half the co2
get to 300 ppm
for a year and a half
and give us a chance to work with new

gadgets and gizmos and gear that won't
poison the air so much,
won't kill us right off,
at least not right away.

We can drop co2 in half,
let the sky do her cleaning then decide
how to change matters
we find out about thereupon.

But it might not be enough after all.

There is another practical matter
that we can parallel pause
for the next seven years.

There are permits to pull

and funding to shift that will stop
one more huge source of choking co2.

One more dial–back
will help us all as pressure goes through
the biggest groups out there.

We can call our government,
our business sector too,
and make it known to all and few
that except for health and medicine
we need to close down
all science
for the next seven years.

Turn all science off,
except health and medicine,

let the sky take a breath,
let the future have a chance.

No driving to the science office,
no air conditioning for science,
no heating for science,
no analyzing data,
no science meetings in another country
that you have to fly to for science.

No research, no spaceships,
no data crunching,
no complex expeditions.

Science is our favorite way
to find out what's already there.

We can wait seven years
to find out what's already there.

The whole point of this is,
we need to make room
for what we invent, everything meant
to reduce our footprints.

The new tech we make will take time to ramp,
it has to come along so slowly,
and even that kicks out
a swing of carbon atoms all along.

Put a seven year stop to the carbon plumes
we already have.

Knock down the measure

to 300 ppm, nice and low
for a year and a half.

Watch what the atmosphere does
at that level.

We have to remember that
every solution adds extra pollution.

Nothing makes less pollution
except nothing.

All science, full stop
for the next seven years.

No labs, no electrons tunneling.

Let scientists plant trees
by hand without using fuel
in every American suburb.

Imagine the acreage, watered and green.

We could see here the first million
new trees all planted by hand
sooner than you could imagine.

No science for seven years.

No research, no atom smashing
that alone uses so much energy
they have to make up new words for it.

The carbon plume from atom smashing,

whenever they fire one off,

is something like ten thousand parking lots

full of muscle cars gunning their engines

all at the same time.

Sixth Thing to Do Won't Make Any Friends

No, no, no, no,
no, no, no, no, no
no Nobel Prize for the next seven years.

Look at the way those giant brains
those wizards, those very smart people
have set up a roasting death,
they've set us up
like rotisserie chickens,
then they hold out their hands, say
Where's my prize?

The way this planet is rigged for now,
nobody gets a Nobel
for the next seven years.

Let the Kings of Norway and Sweden
make a special pronouncement
with parchment scroll and seals attached
that reminds everyone
that they are withholding
all the praise and all the money
for a full seven years.

We all want a better life here but
how can we survive
with the sky like it is these days?

They've been at it for centuries
so now we can see this world of theirs,
their inventions and their progress
is now this world of ours.

This world of theirs and
this world of ours we all made together
and they say our extinction is certain and soon,
then hold out their hands for a prize?

Let them clip a branch off a tree
then plant that wherever they can walk.

Plant a trillion trees by hand.

Ground every plane for the next seven years.

Cut loose the wisdom
of silent teens.

Every City a Dark Sky City
where artists paint cityscapes
with night and with light.

Put a stop to all science
'cept health and medicine
for the next seven years.

No Nobel Prize for the next seven years,
who believes in a prize
as we head for extinction?

Oh yes, we do head for extinction.